ANIMALS HEAD TO HEAD

Polar bear VS. Grizzly bear

This book is dedicated to the memory of Lucy Owen,
who really cared about this series.

ISABEL THOMAS

www.raintreepublishers.co.uk
Visit our website to find out more information about **Raintree** books.

To order:
☎ Phone 44 (0) 1865 888112
📄 Send a fax to 44 (0) 1865 314091
💻 Visit the Raintree bookshop at **www.raintreepublishers.co.uk** to browse our catalogue and order online.

First published in Great Britain by Raintree,
Halley Court, Jordan Hill, Oxford OX2 8EJ,
part of Harcourt Education.
Raintree is a registered trademark
of Harcourt Education Ltd.

Editorial: Dan Nunn and Katie Shepherd
Design: Victoria Bevan
and Bridge Creative Services Ltd
Picture Research: Hannah Taylor
and Rebecca Sodergren
Production: Duncan Gilbert

Originated by Chroma Graphics Pte. Ltd
Printed and bound in China by
South China Printing Company

13 digit ISBN 978 1 406 20330 1 (hardback)
10 09 08 07 06
10 9 8 7 6 5 4 3 2 1

13 digit ISBN 978 1 406 20337 0 (paperback)
11 10 09 08 07
10 9 8 7 6 5 4 3 2 1

**British Library Cataloguing in
Publication Data**
Thomas, Isabel, 1980–
  Polar bear vs. grizzly bear. – (Animals head to head)
  1. Grizzly bear – Juvenile literature
  2. Polar bear – Juvenile literature
  3. Animal fighting – Juvenile literature
  4. Predation (Biology) – Juvenile literature
  I. Title
  599.7'841566
A full catalogue record for this book is available
from the British Library.

Acknowledgements
The publishers would like to thank the following for
permission to reproduce photographs:

Alamy Images pp. **8**, **15** (Robert McGouey), **28**
(Blickwinkel); ardea.com pp. **7** (M. Watson), **26 left**
(M. Watson), **26 right** (M. Watson); Corbis pp. **4
left** (Jim Zuckerman), **10** (Galen Rowell), **18 left**
(Galen Rowell); FLPA/Minden Pictures pp. **4 right**
(Michio Hoshino), **13** (ZSSD), **16** (Matthias Brelter),
17 (Patricio Robles Gil), **22** (Michio Hoshino), **25**
(Michio Hoshino); Getty Images/The Image Bank
pp. **6**, **11**, **21**; Imagestate pp. **23**, **24**; National
Geographic p. **12**; naturepl.com pp. **9** (Sue Flood),
20 (Patricio Robles Gil), **29** (Tom Mangelsen);
Photolibrary.com pp. **14**, **18 right**, **19** (Index
Stock Imagery).

Cover photograph of a grizzly bear reproduced
with permission of Corbis/John Conrad. Cover
photograph of a polar bear reproduced with
permission of Ardea/Doc White .

Every effort has been made to contact copyright
holders of any material reproduced in this book.
Any omissions will be rectified in subsequent
printings if notice is given to the publishers.

The paper used to print this book comes from
sustainable resources.

Disclaimer
All the Internet addresses (URLs) given in this book
were valid at the time of going to press. However,
due to the dynamic nature of the Internet, some
addresses may have changed, or sites may have
changed or ceased to exist since publication. While
the author and publishers regret any inconvenience
this may cause readers, no responsibility for any
such changes can be accepted by either the author
or the publishers.

Contents

Any words appearing in the text in bold, **like this**, are explained in the glossary.

Meet the bears

Spring has arrived. A hungry grizzly bear stumbles out of his forest den and sinks his teeth into a moose that has not survived the cold winter.

Further north, a polar bear waits motionless beside a crack in the ice. When a seal pops up for air, the bear smashes through the ice and yanks its **prey** out of the water.

Polar bears and grizzly bears are **predators**. They survive by hunting and eating other animals. All predators' bodies are designed to help them find, catch, and eat meat.

Most bears try to avoid people, but they can be very dangerous.

Polar bears hunt alone. They get angry if other bears try to steal their food.

4

Bears are the biggest meat-eating land **mammals** in the world. Polar bears **roam** the icy landscapes and frozen seas of the **Arctic**. Grizzlies are a type of brown bear. They live in forests and grasslands in North America.

Grizzlies and polar bears are known and respected as deadly hunters. But which bear is the champion predator? To find out, we need to compare their hunting and fighting skills.

This map shows where grizzlies and polar bears can be found in the wild.

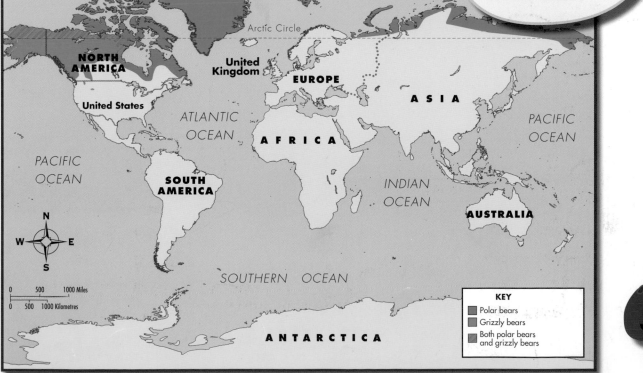

Arctic Circle

NORTH AMERICA

United Kingdom

EUROPE

ASIA

United States

ATLANTIC OCEAN

AFRICA

PACIFIC OCEAN

PACIFIC OCEAN

SOUTH AMERICA

INDIAN OCEAN

AUSTRALIA

N
W   E
S

0   500   1000 Miles
0   500   1000 Kilometres

SOUTHERN OCEAN

ANTARCTICA

KEY
Polar bears
Grizzly bears
Both polar bears and grizzly bears

Size and strength

The biggest **predators** have the best choice of food. Bears hunt alone, using their enormous size and strength to catch large **prey**. Size is also important for attracting females. Only the largest and fiercest males get to **breed**.

Male grizzlies are more than 2 metres (6 feet 7 inches) tall when they stand on their **hind legs**. They stand like this to see what is happening around them. They also stand when they are feeling frightened or angry.

2 m (6 ft 7 in)

Grizzlies are fattest in autumn. Large bears weigh up to 600 kg (1,322 lb).

Polar bears have even larger bodies than grizzlies. Males can grow to lengths of over 3 metres (10 feet) from nose to tail. They can weigh twice as much as a grizzly and fourteen times more than a person!

Polar bears are the largest meat-eating land animals in the world!

3 m (10 ft)

Huge muscles help polar bears and grizzlies to catch food. The hump of muscle on a grizzly's back gives it enough power to break the neck of a young bison.

Polar bears use their strength to smash through cracks in the ice and grab heavy seals. They will even tackle animals as big as beluga whales and walruses.

Some seals hide their pups in snow caves – but even this is not safe. Polar bears break into caves by rising up on their **hind legs** and crashing down on the icy roof with enormous force.

Grizzlies use their strong front legs to flip rocks and logs in their search for tasty insects.

8

The fatter the better

A thick layer of fat makes bears extremely bulky. When food is easy to find, polar bears and grizzlies eat as much as possible, so they get fatter. When food is hard to find, bears live off their stored fat. The fat is stored under the skin, so it also protects the bears from injury and keeps them warm.

Polar bears are so strong they can even attack huge whales.

HEAD TO HEAD

WINNER

	Polar	Grizzly	
Size	10	8	Grizzly is in the polar bear's shadow.
Strength	10	9	Polar bear muscles its way to victory.

Speed and stamina

A **predator's** body is designed for its **habitat**. Polar bears are closely related to grizzlies, but look different because they have **adapted** to the harsh **Arctic** habitat.

Both bears are fast runners, but only polar bears can sprint on ice. Small bumps and tufts of hair on their paws grip the ice. This allows them to chase **prey** at up to 40 kph (25 mph).

Grizzlies might look slow, but a charging grizzly can actually run at over 50 kph (31 mph). This is fast enough to keep up with a galloping horse!

Grizzlies can run much faster than humans. The only escape is to climb a tree.

Polar bears can easily get too hot, so they usually walk slowly. Food is hard to find in the Arctic, so polar bears have to cover huge distances in their search for food. They can sometimes travel 80 kilometres (50 miles) in one day!

Swimming and diving

Bears are great swimmers. Polar bears can paddle more than 100 kilometres (62 miles) without taking a break. Huge webbed paws pull them through the water. Polar bears can hold their breath underwater for about 2 minutes. This is useful for catching prey and swimming under ice.

A polar bear's territory is up to 350 times bigger than a grizzly's.

Endurance

Polar bears do most of their hunting early in the day. When they are not hunting, they rest or sleep to save energy. Grizzlies are active day and night in summer, but they spend the winter resting.

Surviving without food

A **hibernating** grizzly survives for six months or more without eating or drinking. Its heartbeat and breathing slow down to save energy. Stored body fat keeps the bear alive as it dozes in a warm den. Female polar bears sleep through the **Arctic** summer, when food is harder to catch. But male polar bears do not hibernate.

Grizzlies spend over half their lives dozing in their den.

Temperature control

The Arctic air temperature can fall to −34°C (−29°F) in winter. Even in summer the temperature does not rise above 0°C (32°F). Polar bears are so well **adapted** to their frozen **habitat** that they often get too hot!

Their muscles heat up when they move, just like ours. But thick fur and a layer of **blubber** stop this heat from escaping. The bears rub themselves on patches of ice and snow to cool down.

A layer of blubber keeps polar bears warm as they swim in icy Arctic seas.

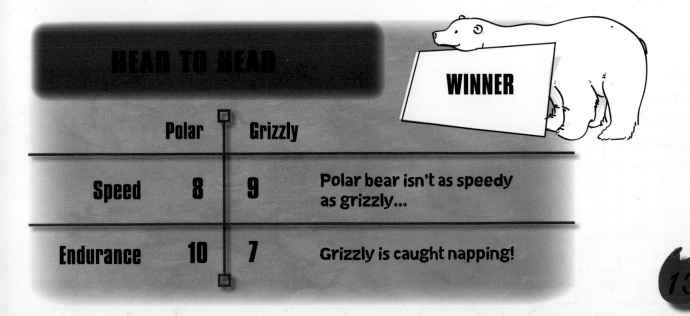

HEAD TO HEAD

WINNER

	Polar	Grizzly	
Speed	8	9	Polar bear isn't as speedy as grizzly...
Endurance	10	7	Grizzly is caught napping!

A surprise attack

A **predator's senses** are designed for hunting. Bears have good eyesight and hearing, but they are best known for their sense of smell. This is important because bears hunt over huge areas, so they need to know which way to go to find **prey**.

Nosing around

Polar bears are thought to have the most sensitive noses in the world. On a windy day in the **Arctic** they can smell a seal that is 30 kilometres (18 miles) away. They can even find seal dens hidden under metres of snow.

A bear's big nose is a sign that it uses smell to find prey.

14

Nothing goes to waste

Grizzlies can sniff out food from several kilometres away. Their noses are good at finding prey amongst all the other forest smells. They like the smell of dead animals, which make an easy meal.

Hungry grizzlies and polar bears are also attracted to the smell of food in human rubbish. This means they often try to find food in waste dumps and bins.

If bears get too close to houses, they risk being killed by frightened people.

Creeping up on prey

Most **predators** use amazing skills of **stealth** to **ambush** their victims.

Cunning **camouflage** keeps bears hidden as they approach their **prey**. Polar bears are completely covered in fur, apart from their nose and footpads. Each hair is a tiny, **transparent** tube. The hairs reflect light and make the polar bear look white. This helps it to blend in with the snow and ice in its **habitat**.

A polar bear's fur is excellent camouflage in an icy habitat.

With fur that blends in with the habitat, a grizzly can get close to prey without being noticed.

A grizzly's thick, shaggy fur helps it to look even bigger when it wants to scare enemies. Some grizzlies have white-tipped or "grizzled" fur, which gives them their name.

Waterproof fur

Oil from a bear's skin makes sure its fur doesn't clump together as it swims. When a bear climbs out of the water, it shakes itself dry like a dog.

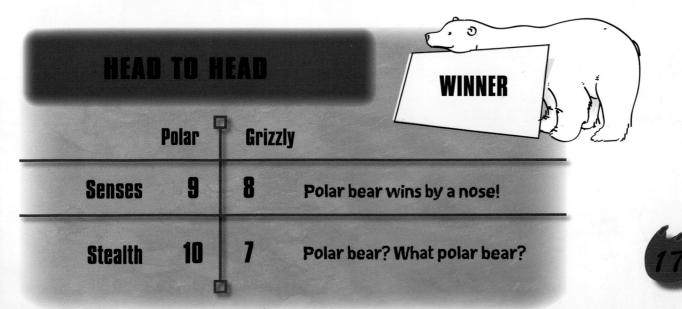

HEAD TO HEAD

WINNER

	Polar	Grizzly	
Senses	9	8	Polar bear wins by a nose!
Stealth	10	7	Polar bear? What polar bear?

Claws and jaws

All **predators** have special weapons to help catch and kill **prey**. Claws are designed for gripping and tearing things.

Tools for every task

A grizzly's 10 cm (4 inch) front claws are useful for grabbing big animals and skewering salmon. But they are mainly used for digging up roots, insects or berries. Grizzlies also scratch tree trunks to warn other bears to stay away. Grizzly paws are flexible enough to unscrew jars and open car doors to find food.

A grizzly's huge paws can break an animal's neck with one blow.

Snow shoes

Polar bear paws are also huge. They spread out the bear's weight, so its legs do not sink into the snow or crack thin ice. When the ice is very thin, a polar bear will crawl on its belly to spread its weight out even more.

A polar bear's thick, curved claws are used for grabbing prey and fighting rivals. They also stop the bear from slipping as it runs or climbs on ice.

A polar bear's paw can be 30 cm (12 inches) wide.

19

Sharp canine teeth easily tear through tough skin.

Bite force

Polar bears and grizzlies have 42 teeth. Like all **carnivores**, they have four sharp **canines**. These are used for grabbing and killing **prey**. Bears have strong jaw muscles, which help their teeth to deliver a savage bite.

A polar bear's front teeth and sharp side teeth cut off pieces of **blubber** and flesh, while large back teeth crunch and grind. Most food is swallowed in bite-sized chunks.

Grizzlies are **omnivores**. They eat plants as well as meat. Most omnivores don't have very sharp canines, but grizzlies do! They are useful for killing prey, scaring off rivals, and ripping open trees to find insects.

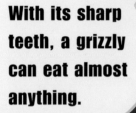

With its sharp teeth, a grizzly can eat almost anything.

HEAD TO HEAD

WINNER

	Polar	Grizzly	
Claws	7	8	Grizzly finds more uses for claws and paws.
Jaws	8	8	Both bites are deadly.

Hunting skills

Polar bears are expert hunters. Sensitive noses help them find food in one of the toughest **habitats** in the world.

They can even sniff out seals' breathing holes. When a seal comes up for air, the bear crashes through the hole and kills its **prey** with a single bite. It uses its powerful claws to rip the seal apart.

Polar bears also hunt seals that are basking on land. They creep close and then charge, pinning down their victim with a massive paw.

Polar bears need to wait patiently for a seal to appear.

Unfussy eaters

Grizzlies do not hunt big prey as often as polar bears do. Just a quarter of their food is meat. They eat small **mammals**, such as newborn deer and ground squirrels. Grizzlies also catch fish with a quick snap of their jaws, or by pinning them down with their paws.

Most of a grizzly's day is spent eating leaves, fungi, and berries. One bear can eat 200,000 berries in a day!

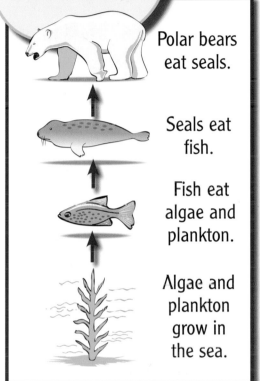

A food chain shows who eats what in a habitat.

Polar bears eat seals.

Seals eat fish.

Fish eat algae and plankton.

Algae and plankton grow in the sea.

Young cubs learn to hunt and fight by wrestling their brothers and sisters.

Grizzly vs. wolf
In Yellowstone National Park in the United States, large male grizzlies have been seen stealing food from a pack of wolves!

Battling bears

Polar bears and grizzlies are excellent fighters. Sharp **senses** make it hard for other animals to sneak up on them. Enormous bodies, claws, and teeth are deadly weapons.

Food fight

Bears don't bother to defend their huge **territories**. But they get very angry if another bear tries to steal their **prey**. A deep growl warns other bears to stay away.

Every year dozens of grizzlies gather at the same rivers to catch salmon. The biggest, most threatening males win the best fishing spots.

These wrestling bears are trying to bite each other.

24

Fight for the right to breed

Male polar bears are very competitive when they want to attract females. The biggest males show off their strength by hissing and standing on their **hind legs**.

If a rival does not run away, the bears wrestle. Fighting is dangerous because it can lead to wounds or even death.

Polar bears hiss, growl, and snap their teeth together when they are angry.

Ferocious females

Female bears are most ferocious when they are looking after babies. Hungry males see cubs as a tasty snack, so the mother is always ready to attack.

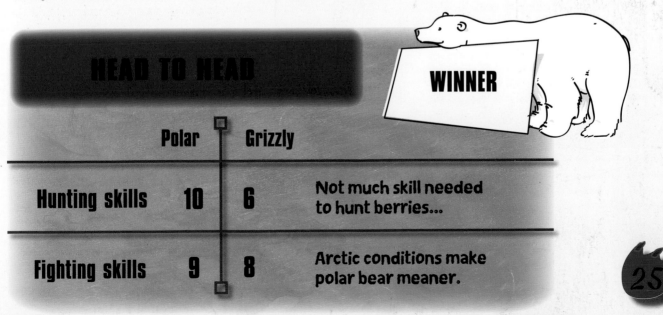

HEAD TO HEAD

WINNER

	Polar	Grizzly	
Hunting skills	10	6	Not much skill needed to hunt berries...
Fighting skills	9	8	Arctic conditions make polar bear meaner.

Who wins?

A super **sense** of smell, powerful bodies, and sharp teeth make bears fantastic **predators**. But which bear is best? Let's imagine what might happen if they met...

Bear encounter

Male bears are most likely to fight over food. They would try to warn each other off by lowering their heads, growling, and baring their teeth.

If neither bear backed down, they might stand on their **hind legs** and wrestle. Each bear would bite and scratch his rival's head and neck.

These huge **mammals** would be well matched. Grizzlies are some of the most dangerous animals in North America. But polar bears grow up to a metre longer and are tough enough to swim across freezing oceans. Grizzlies spend most of their time eating plants, but polar bears often hunt massive whales, walruses, and reindeer.

Faced with the power and killing skills of a polar bear, a grizzly would be wise to run away.

HEAD TO HEAD

	Polar	Grizzly
Size	10	8
Strength	10	9
Speed	8	9
Endurance	10	7
Senses	9	8
Stealth	10	7
Claws	7	8
Jaws	8	8
Hunting skills	10	6
Fighting skills	9	8
Total	91/100	78/100

Polar bear proves to be the coolest champion!

The real fight

Grizzly bears and polar bears do not often meet in the wild. But they have a worse enemy to fear – humans.

Humans destroy bear **territories** by building houses, cutting down trees, and drilling for oil and gas. They kill bears for meat and fur, or because they are afraid. They **pollute** bear **habitats** with rubbish and poisonous chemicals.

Room to roam

Grizzlies once lived in most of North America, but now they are found only in Canada, Alaska, and a few parts of the northwest United States. It is against the law to hunt grizzlies, but sadly they are still at risk.

Roads that cut through national parks are a big threat to grizzlies.

Forty years ago just 10,000 polar bears were alive. Then the five countries where polar bears live (Canada, Greenland, Norway, the United States, and Russia) agreed to protect these important animals and their habitat. The population has grown to 22,000, but polar bears are still **endangered**.

Walking on thin ice

The biggest threat to polar bears is **global warming**. The **Arctic** sea ice is disappearing. Polar bears need sea ice to hunt. They are already getting smaller and having fewer cubs.

These awesome **predators** will only survive if everyone treats them, and their habitats, with the respect they deserve.

Global warming is melting the Arctic ice and destroying the polar bear's habitat.

Glossary

adapt to change over time to suit the conditions in a certain habitat

ambush to attack prey suddenly, from a hiding place

Arctic area of the world that lies around the North Pole

blubber thick layer of fat under the skin of some large mammals, such as whales and polar bears, which keeps them warm

breed to have babies

camouflage body features that allow animals to blend into their habitat, to avoid being seen by predators or prey

canines sharp pointed teeth at the front of the mouth. Most mammals have four canines.

carnivore animal that mainly eats other animals

endangered in danger of dying out altogether

global warming way that human actions are causing the world's temperature to rise

habitat place where an animal lives

hibernate to become less active over the winter, living off only body fat

hind legs back legs of an animal that walks on four legs

mammal animal that can make its own body heat and produce milk for its babies

omnivore animal that eats many different kinds of food, including plants and other animals

pollute damage an area of air, land or water

predator animal that hunts, kills, and eats other animals

prey animal that is caught, killed, and eaten by another animal as food

roam move over a large area

senses ways in which an animal gets information about its surroundings

stealth doing something slowly and quietly to avoid being noticed

territory area that an animal lives in and defends against rivals

transparent material that lets light pass through it

More information

Books

Dangerous Creatures, Angela Wilkes (Kingfisher, 2003) will help you find out more about bears and other deadly animals.

Why am I a mammal?, Greg Pyers (Raintree, 2005) will tell you more about bear biology.

Wild Predators: Killer Carnivores, Andrew Solway (Heinemann Library, 2005) explores the lives of the most dangerous meat-eaters, including enormous bears.

Websites

www.nationalgeographic.com/kids – visit this site and search for "bears" to find photos and facts about these awesome animals.

www.bbc.co.uk/reallywild – this site is packed with facts, features, and games. Follow the "mammals" link to learn more about bears, or click on "creature close-up" to get really close to a polar bear!

www.polarbearsinternational.org – this site has hundreds of facts about polar bears.

www.nwf.org/wildlife/grizzlybear/ – visit this site to become a grizzly bear expert with its amazing facts and photos.

Sizing up the polar bear and grizzly bear

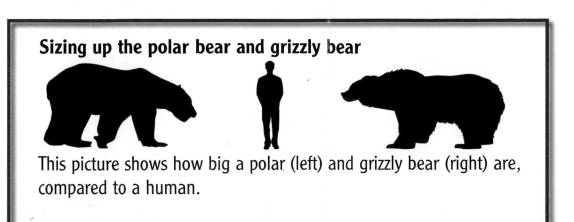

This picture shows how big a polar (left) and grizzly bear (right) are, compared to a human.

Index